BY THE EDITORS OF CONSUMER GUIDE®

MODEL PLANES

Beekman House

New York

Contents

This edition published by:
Beekman House
A Division of Crown Publishers, Inc.
One Park Avenue
New York, N.Y. 10016

Library of Congress Catalog Card Number: 79-64871
ISBN: 0-517-294575

Introduction

1

THE ROMANCE OF FLIGHT and the lore of things that fly have been with us for centuries. The heroes and heroines of ancient Greek and Roman myths were said to soar high in the skies on sometimes man-made, sometimes heavenly wings. Elaborate kites were designed and flown in Asian festivals more than 2000 years ago. Leonardo da Vinci drew detailed plans for gliders and people-powered aircraft in the early 1500s. Two hundred years later, Benjamin Franklin used tethered flying craft in a variety of scientific experiments and to tow small boats and rafts across water. Hot-air and gas-filled balloons were used to lift people into the sky for short but daring journeys. Then came Sir George Cayley's research into aerodynamics, the Lilienthal brothers' pioneering glider flight, and finally the airplane.

The age of the powered airplane began at Kitty

If your interest is in biplanes from the World War I era, you'll be able to select a plastic model for display (1) or a larger model that flies (3). Free-flight models come in many different configurations (2). No matter what type of model building you intend to do, you will be limited only by your budget, your skills and your imagination.

Hawk, North Carolina, on December 17, 1903, when Orville Wright took off and piloted the Wright brothers' crude but functional craft on an eight-second flight at a peak altitude of 12 feet. From there, our mastery of the skies grew explosively: along came biplanes, monoplanes, helicopters, seaplanes, fighter planes, long-range bombers, supersonic jets and jumbo jets. The names of modern-day heroes and heroines like Charles Lind-

bergh, Amelia Earhart and Billy Mitchell became household words. An industry was born, and other names like Boeing, McDonnell-Douglas and Lockheed, United, American, TWA and Pan American took to the sky.

Although the airplane has become a commonplace member of the world's transportation community, it has never lost its glamor or excitement. The airplane was once a vehicle of daring. Going up in one in the early days took courage — perhaps a sense of abandon. It was, in those days, a phenomenon that entertained and awed us as we watched barnstormers and stunt fliers perform their dazzling feats in the sky. Today, even for those of us who are not daredevils, the airplane is still a vehicle of romance that takes us quickly and comfortably to places far away. The world is ever more dependent upon the airplane, in peace and at war.

Testament to the world's respect and fascination for airplanes is the fact that as the airplane developed, the leisure-time construction of scale-model airplanes of a staggering variety — some for ornamentation, others that could fly — took its place as one of the most popular hobbies in the world. It has

gathered fans of all ages: children and adults who are casual modelers, and skilled artisans who devote weeks to working out infinitesimal details of exact scale replicas.

The building of small flying machines actually was popular long before piloted craft were developed. Throughout the 1800s, these little planes were fashioned in Europe and the United States for scientific experimentation as well as for recreation. Technically, they were not models because they were not replicas of existing airplanes. Instead, they were unique creations, springing from the craftsman's imagination and investigation of aerodynamic principles. They were not copies, but forerunners of the real thing.

Today, millions of people throughout the world

1

2

3

involve themselves in one form or another of model aircrafting. They spend millions of dollars on kits, tools, paints, engines and control devices.

Model aeronautics includes two different activities: building the model airplanes and flying them. Both are almost limitless as to what can be accomplished; both involve learning, practice, experimentation and the honing of skills. They are hobbies in which expertise develops through effort and experience. It would be unwise, for example, to choose an extremely detailed and complex model as your first project, or to jump right into a top-level combat contest on your first flight with a radio-controlled model.

But model airplaning is a hobby and a craft in which almost everyone can move ahead with sur- prising speed and facility. As a result, it is usually not long before you can build extremely complex and impressive models or are able to manipulate your airplane in flight with great dexterity.

Model Planes describes in great detail each of these forms of model aircrafting, shows how you can get started in this entertaining hobby and illustrates what you can accomplish. This is also a source book for organizations and suppliers of the necessary equipment. Whether you have a mind to break altitude records with your planes or just spend Sunday afternoons flying one leisurely around a park, to build models with engines or concentrate on winged works of art designed for display, this book is intended to prepare you for a smooth take-off.

4

5

Radio-control fans have a choice of planes such as the engine-powered Lanier Dart (1) or an engineless glider from Cox (3). Even though they build models that fly, many RC pilots spend countless hours creating astonishingly detailed works of art (2). Those who have a great deal of experience in model flying accumulate boxes full of accessories and spare parts (4). There is a thrill in sending even the simplest plane into the sky (5).

CHARTING YOUR FLIGHT PLAN is the first step in becoming a model aircraft hobbyist. Will you build models for display or for flying? Will you assemble flying models from kits or buy them ready-made? For an overview of what types of products are available in this wide-ranging hobby, you can visit a local hobby shop, write for information and contact one of the large organizations of model fanciers.

In many cases, the employees of hobby shops can provide you with expert advice on the different forms of model airplanes. They can recommend starter kits and give you an idea of the assortment of products to be considered. Their experience with a particular brand of models, for instance, may help you decide which companies to contact directly for more information.

Model airplane and equipment manufacturers publish catalogs. These illustrate the array of models and supplies available from the makers and tell

Getting Started

you what they cost. The models vary widely in price, authenticity and overall quality, so this can be a good way to do some comparative shopping. There are also several magazines and other publications for the modeler which offer everything from advice about assembly to calendars of upcoming competitions.

Two excellent sources for the beginner are the International Plastic Model Society for static-model builders and the Academy of Model Aeronautics for flying-model enthusiasts. Both of these organizations can provide basic guidance as well as the means to contact clubs in your locale.

After you have decided which type of model aircraft you will work with, another decision is important: you probably will want to choose a particular scale.

Models are normally identified by the scale to which they will be built; that is, the size of the model in proportion to the real aircraft. One model

2

3

4

If you decide to build flying models, the possibilities are endless. You can construct beautiful radio-controlled models that will attract crowds at RC meets (1). You can buy small engines such as those made by Cox (2) and install them in a variety of planes that you build yourself, or buy control-line models from Cox (3) and other companies that are ready to fly just as they come from the box. As you progress in the hobby of flying models, you may want to build planes that not only perform well in flight, but also closely resemble the full-size craft. To do that, many modelers take great care to paint their planes with authentic colors, and even make them look weather-beaten (4).

1

2

Many planes that have become a permanent part of aeronautic history are available in kit form from makers of plastic static models. They include Howard Hughes' Spruce Goose from Entex (1) and the World War I Spad from Revell (2). Radio-control flying models seen at meets come in all shapes and sizes (3). Control-line planes such as the Cox PT-19 Trainer (4) are often the first flying models a beginning hobbyist pilots. Cox also makes free-flight helicopter models (5).

might be marked 1:72; another might be 1:500. The scale means that one inch on the model represents 72 inches on the full-size aircraft in the first case and 500 inches in the second case.

Display and Flight

The building of static replicas is by far the more popular of the two types of model aeronautics. It often begins with the plastic kits for small children. It can extend to the very complicated kits designed for teenagers and adults who are blessed with patience, skill and determination, who can use sophisticated tools and invest in a stock of top-quality supplies. The types of kits presently on the market can boggle the mind of even the most imaginative aviationist. In this form of model airplane building, the hobbyist can re-create in exact-scale detail

3

4

5

practically every type of aircraft ever made, whether it is the Wright Brothers' flimsy biplane, the early Jenny, Howard Hughes' Spruce Goose, the supersonic Concorde or any military plane that fought on either side of any war from World War I to Vietnam.

The art of static models is not limited to the construction of a model airplane: display of those models has become an art in itself. Many models are still simply hung with string from the ceiling, attached to a stand or just set down on a mantel or shelf. However, many modelers create dioramas—realistic scenes—to show off their models. These total environments often are complete with models of people, trees and buildings. In a military diorama, for example, the model airplane may be purposely abused so that it will fit into the scene of a crash landing. Dioramas are available in kit form, but they can be adapted and redesigned. Some are made from scratch.

If you feel restricted by immobile models and want to take to the sky, there is a wide variety of aircraft models that fly—inexpensive ones and very costly ones. Some are assembled from raw materials, some come in kit form and some are available completely assembled for those who are more in-terested in flying than in building. They come in various sizes and are powered in different ways.

Just as the full-scale glider preceded the full-scale motorized aircraft, so too did glider mod-els come before powered ones. The reason is sim-plicity. A glider needs no internal source of power; it can remain aloft with no aid other than air cur-

1

2

Aside from the fact that they all fly, the craft flown by model airplane enthusiasts have little in common. Some of them are biplanes modeled after the dogfighters of World War I (1). In many cases, the techniques used in building these replicas are much the same as those which were used in building the full-size plane. Some flying models are much simpler in construction, having only a slab of balsa or plastic for wings and a small rubber band for power (2). On the other end of the scale are superbly crafted models that utilize space-age technology and powerful jet engines to startle observers with their realistic appearance and flight performance (3).

rents. The glider is often the first flying model that beginning hobbyists put together and fly. But building and flying a glider can be more than mere child's play. You will see that clearly in the chapter devoted to making, launching and flying model gliders. Gliders, like other flying models, compete in a variety of official contests.

Powered models, on the other hand, include everything from "U-control," tethered craft controlled from the ground by a cable or a line, to elaborate radio-controlled models that use sophisticated electronic apparatus that can cost hundreds of dollars. Some U-control models are powered by engines within the aircraft; some by outside

3

1

There are many large organizations of model airplane fanciers, and they often sponsor events that draw hobbyists from miles around. These contests enable modelers to compete with one another in racing their RC planes (1) and to exchange assembly tips (2). At some of the meets, hobbyists will be able to watch gliders take to the air (3) and rubber-powered craft taxi down the runway (4). Often there are buildings or tents available to beginning modelers who want the opportunity to work on their planes under the watchful eyes of experts (5). Many events are held indoors. These include contests for the extremely fragile and light indoor rubber-powered planes (6). Whether you go to compete or to watch, meetings such as these will show you the diverse aircraft built and flown by your fellow hobbyists.

2

3

4

5

6

sources. The powered ones can use rubber bands, internal combustion engines, or even jet engines.

Elaborate radio-controlled, or RC, models are either gliders or powered craft, guided by transmitters that vary greatly in sophistication, effectiveness and cost. RC models are the most widely tested in contests and competitions. They have racked up some impressive world records: Two men in the USSR flew an RC model at the astonishing speed of 213.7 miles per hour; and an American, Maynard Hill, guided an RC model to an altitude of almost 27,000 feet—more than five miles above the earth.

You may never feel the urge to try to break records like those, but you may desire to enter your planes in some type of competition. There are numerous events—many, perhaps, in your area—that enable model aircraft enthusiasts to show each other what they have learned.

There are competitions on the national and local levels for both static models and flying models. A huge variety of events for skills of all types are available, with guidelines, rules, procedures and specifications published by the IPMS and the AMA. Both organizations sanction various competitions and meets. You can write to them for rules and procedures. There are also many other competitions that are not necessarily sanctioned by these groups but have emerged from the imagination and whim of model aviators.

Static Models

1

THE FUN of static airplane models is in building them and displaying the finished product. In the past, static models were made only of wood; today they can be constructed from wood, plastic, or a combination of the two. Plastic airplane model kits are by far the most popular because they can be inexpensively produced with great detail.

The variety of plastic kits available for building static models is vast. They range from simple mod-

els with only a few pieces to elaborate models with hundreds of parts in astonishing detail. More airplane models are currently available than any other type of plastic model: a stop at any hobby or toy shop will show what a truly large selection there is.

For the first attempt at building a static airplane model, it is wise to select one of the less complicated types—one that is not designed for the experienced hobbyist. While building basic models

2

The vast assortment of static model kits includes many early military aircraft. Among the history-making planes of World War I is Baron von Richthoven's Fokker Triplane (1), from Revell. An early American biplane that was put to civilian use is the Boeing F4B-4 (3), from Monogram. Testor's line of aircraft models includes a selection of some very simple kits (2). In modeling these and all other planes, great attention to detail is necessary if the plane is to closely resemble the original. Many hobbyists do a lot of research to make certain that their paint jobs match those of the original planes.

3

is not difficult, there is a definite skill required which a person develops with practice and patience.

Generally speaking, the more pieces there are in a kit, the more detail there is and the longer it will take to assemble it. Most plastic kits on the market today are made to scale from 1:24 to 1:72. However, 1:144 is often the scale for models of large commercial jet airliners, and microscale models as small as 1:500 are available. For your first model or two, you may want to try a model at the scale of 1:48 — not simple enough to be boring, but not too difficult for the novice. As you gain experience and feel comfortable assembling these models, you may want to go on to other scales. Many hobbyists, once they have learned the necessary skills, select a scale and stick with it so that all the models they build will be in scale with each other.

Preparation

When you shop for a plastic model, you will find that the boxes are almost always wrapped so that they cannot be tampered with in the store. This prevents you from examining the contents before purchasing a kit, but keeps it intact until you get it home. A missing piece can cause a good deal of frustration when you are in the middle of assembling the model, so it is wise to avoid buying any box that is not sealed.

Once you get your kit home, one of the first steps is to prepare a place where you can work on the model without interruption and where the pieces will not be disturbed until the model is completed. If you have to gather up or move the parts repeatedly, you will increase the chance of losing them, and glued or painted parts may not dry properly.

In the kit, you will find an instruction sheet listing all the components of the model and giving numbered, step-by-step directions for assembly. The sheet may also give basic suggestions for finishing the airplane, including paint, decals and display. Planning is important, especially for more-complex models. For example, many a modeler has discovered that it is easier to paint certain parts like the inside of a wheel and backside of a propeller before assembly.

Before beginning assembly of the model, take some time to familiarize yourself with the various parts and the directions for putting them together. Some kits, for instance, may offer two or three alternative modifications or choices of how the model can be assembled. In such a case, you may have extra pieces that are not needed according to one set of instructions.

Once you have thoroughly studied the directions, one other preparatory step is required: be sure you have all the necessary tools, supplies and materials at hand.

Assembly

The first assembly step involves cutting and filing the plastic pieces so that the edges are smooth and will fit together properly. The larger plastic pieces usually are loose in the box, but smaller ones often are connected to a plastic "tree." The small pieces are removed from the tree as they are needed. Cut them off carefully with your hobby knife and then shave or sand off the excess plastic. Basic assembly then follows, including fitting the pieces together, cementing parts in place, letting the cemented

1

2

A look of realism is most important to experienced modelers. A painstaking job of painting results in a model that can fool the eye. The DC-10 from Revell, for example (1), has been superimposed on a photograph of sky, and it looks like the full-size aircraft. The propeller of Captain Roy Brown's Sopwith Camel (3) has been painted to resemble real wood for an added touch of authenticity. It too is made by Revell. For a very high level of realism, many hobbyists create whole scenes in which to display their planes. Called dioramas, these landscapes show what the aircraft looks like in various situations. The diorama of the World War II Black Widow (2), created by Monogram, shows the aging bomber being repaired in the desert.

3

1

2

parts dry thoroughly and putting the cracks.

The only required equipment for assembling a model airplane is a model-maker's knife or single-edge razor blade, fine sandpaper and cement. You can get by with that, but it will not make your work easy. Additional supplies can help you add finishing touches to make your model a standout. Some of this equipment can be found around the house. Additional knife blades of different sizes and shapes for different or specialized tasks are useful and a small investment you will not regret.

You probably will not have to worry about accumulating the extras until you get into very complex models or sophisticated adaptations and redesigns.

Follow the kit directions closely. Some parts have slots and projections that fit together into a smooth assembly, so be sure you do not accidentally trim these away. Always work slowly and carefully as you trim away excess plastic: it can be very difficult to repair a piece of plastic that has been overcut.

The glue or cement to be used in the assembly of

To do justice to the sleek lines of the Gates Lear jet (1), the modeler gave it a perfectly smooth paint job and added details with decals. It is a Testor kit. The Mirage fighter, (2), is used by the Israeli air force, so care was taken to match paint colors to those used on the life-size version. It is from Revell. Monogram makes a model of the Mustang F-51D (3), complete with decals that enable the modeler to duplicate original markings. Another Monogram diorama (4) shows the company's model of the B-24-J Liberator with a unique paint scheme. It is decorated as it would have been to serve as a target tow plane.

3

4

your model should be selected carefully. Regular household glue does not dry quickly enough, and glue used for wooden models will not work properly on plastic ones. A special type of cement called solvent adhesive is necessary for assembling plastic models. This plastic cement, available in metal tubes and bottles, will slightly dissolve part of the two plastic surfaces that are to be joined. Obviously, this type of adhesive must be handled carefully and sparingly: wiping away excess cement can dissolve and damage other parts of the model's surface.

It is often best to apply cement from a tube with a toothpick so that you can add only a drop or two at a time. The bottled glue comes with a brush. Most plastic cements set fairly quickly. This helps speed up assembly, because you must wait until each joint is completely dry before moving on to the next step. It is also very important to set the joint exactly: once the cement has hardened, it is virtually impossible to change. All seams or joints should be filled with model putty and sanded smooth.

Decoration

When the model is completely assembled, you can leave it as it is with only the molded details showing, or add decals, paint and other decorations to give it the desired degree of authenticity. You can get a basic idea for painting and decorating the model by studying the picture on the box. There also may be illustrations and suggestions on the instruction sheet or elsewhere in the kit. Researching the history of a particular model and planning how to decorate it is, however, the highlight of the whole process to many model builders. It can provide a most dramatic and graphic result.

The first step in decoration, as in assembly, is planning. As part of that planning, you must select appropriate paints. Paint for models is available at most hobby shops. There is a very large selection of colors to choose from. Be sure to buy enamel made for use with plastic models. Also, be certain that the brushes you select are good ones: artist-type brushes will not shed hairs; inexpensive brushes

1

Models from all periods of the plane's development are available. Monogram makes a 1:48 scale kit of the huge B-29 Flying Fortress used by the U.S. in World War II (1). Thousands of Monogram's model of the Wright brothers' biplane (2) have been purchased by the Smithsonian Institution. Revell's Spad XIII (3) has been painted to resemble the plane flown by Eddie Rickenbacker, America's World War I ace. America's F-4E Phantom II (4) is a modern jet fighter/bomber. The kit is made by Revell.

2

tend to shed and will cause problems. Before painting, be sure to wash the model thoroughly with soap and water to remove any grease, dirt or other materials that may have collected during assembly.

It is best to apply an undercoat of paint to the model before the actual cover coat: this seals porous areas and points out any defects that you will want to fix before applying the final coat of paint. When your paint job is complete and thoroughly dry, you can then apply decals that came with the kit or others available at hobby shops.

3

4

Many a child's room, family room or basement is decorated with a model airplane hanging by a string or thread from the ceiling. Some are displayed on stands. As a collection grows, however, more thought must be given to how to display your handiwork. Bookshelves often are used as display cases and a small wad of modeling clay can hold the model in a desired position.

Dioramas

The diorama is an intriguing method of displaying models. These dioramas, shadow boxes or total environments limit the number of aircraft which can be displayed, but they can present a realistic and dramatic scene.

Displaying airplane models in a realistic diorama is a craft in itself. It is a truly imaginative one, and the results are the products of the creator's ingenuity and talents. Kits are available from some manufacturers, but most of it is really up to you. You can get ideas for diorama displays by looking through magazines and books that show aircraft in action scenes—with ground crews servicing the aircraft, after a crash landing, or whatever your research and imagination can develop. The skills required are no more complicated than those required for ordinary scale-model building. The materials needed to build a diorama generally can be found around the house or at hobby shops.

The first step—just as in building an airplane model—is to plan what you want to create. Again, when starting out, it is best to keep your display fairly simple. Get ideas from pictures or stories and use your own imagination, but keep in mind the limitations of your equipment and supplies.

Once the idea for your diorama is planned, gather up the model and all the rest of the equipment and materials for the display. Then determine just how much space will be required for the exhibit. Measure carefully the size and shape you will need for a base, allowing for a 3/4-inch margin around the entire diorama. Then cut a base from half-inch plywood. You may wish to frame the base with molding or veneer tape to give your diorama a handsome finished look.

The terrain of your diorama can be covered with papier-mâché or a similar material found at art supply stores. The material is mixed with water and applied to the base. Sand and tiny pebbles can then be sprinkled on the wet surface to give the appearance of ground. Sawdust or hemp rope fibers, dyed with food coloring, can be used to simulate grass. To make a concrete runway for your diorama, you can use a rough posterboard which can be painted to your liking. A glue syringe is a perfect applicator for small details. Be sure to give the runway realism by making it look weathered and by adding such touches as the appearance of oil spills.

Additional figures and equipment can add a great deal to the interest of your scene. Models of service

1

2

vehicles can often be found at hobby shops or toy stores. Boxes and crates can be made from small blocks of wood or fashioned from cardboard. Ladders, fuel drums and tools can also add to the effect. If you wish to show a section of the aircraft open, remember that you will need to do some research to make sure the internal parts that will be exposed are authentic looking.

You will also want to give the airplane itself the appearance of weathering. A plane that has been in service—one perhaps that has crashed—obviously will not have the fresh-colored paint it did when it left the factory. The upper sides which have been exposed to the sun will be lighter than the undersides. There will also be areas of chipped paint and oil stains. Artist's chalk, powdered and applied with a soft brush, is one method that can be used to produce a weathered effect. A more lasting method

is to apply weathering by painting with a water-base paint over the original enamel using a lighter color.

To give the appearance that the aircraft is actually resting on the ground, you can flatten the bottom of each tire. If the diorama is of a crash scene, more than just weathering will be necessary. The effect of bullet holes can be added by piercing the plastic with the point of a hot knife or needle. Propellers can be bent out of shape if heat is cautiously applied. A knife or hand grinder can be used to create torn and jagged wings or to illustrate other damage to the fuselage. Any exposed internal sections will have to be created from scratch. Similarly, the ground area will have to reflect the devastation that would normally be caused by an airplane crash.

Attention to detail is very important in creating an

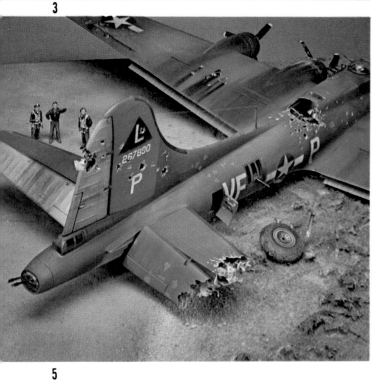

Monogram's model of the B-17G bomber can be built to show what the plane looked like when new (1), but many modelers may find that it is more fun to build a realistic diorama for the plane (2). To create such a work of art, modelers study all aspects of the plane's construction so they can fabricate damaged interior components from scratch. Miniature figures, bed rolls made from facial tissue and earth made of papier-mâché complete the picture (3, 4, 5).

effective diorama. When all parts are properly prepared, each piece is attached to the base of the diorama with glue. When you are finished, you will have a unique creation that goes a step beyond simple static model making.

THE BASICS

Hobby knife with additional blades or single-edge razor blades
Sandpaper (No. 500)
Scissors
Jeweler's files
Spring clothespins
Rubber bands
Toothpicks
Cotton-tipped swabs
Tweezers

Rags
Masking tape
Cement (liquid and tube)
Model putty
Enamel paint (bottles and/or spray cans)
Paint brushes (Sable Nos. 001, 1, 3)
Brush cleaner
Decals

THE EXTRAS

Jeweler's screwdrivers
Jeweler's vise
Small power drill
C-clamps
Bulldog clips
Additional paint brushes
Air brush

Gliders

1

PEOPLE HAVE BEEN flying in glider planes ever since 1891 when Otto and Gustav Lilienthal made the first successful piloted glider flight. However, people had fashioned and flown smaller gliders centuries before that for sport and experimentation. Interest in man-size gliders for recreation and research has grown steadily over the decades. Gliders carry a pilot skyward for flights of several hours in the sport of soaring.

Interest in model gliders also has continued to grow. These models include all forms of planes from the simple little balsa ones which have entertained children for generations to radio-controlled sailplanes with wingspans of ten feet or more. There are competitions for fans of the most basic "pennyplanes," the large RC models and everything in between. The little planes can still be found in drugstores and toy shops; the big ones are available from manufacturers who make kits for advanced hobbyists.

The very inexpensive and simple gliders for the beginner are usually made of balsa just as they were many years ago. Others are made of lightweight plastics. In most cases, the only assembly required is insertion of precut wings and stabilizers into their slots in the plane's body. There may not be much to putting one together, but it takes skill to send one on a prize-winning flight.

Other, larger gliders present a real challenge to their builders right from the first step of assembly.

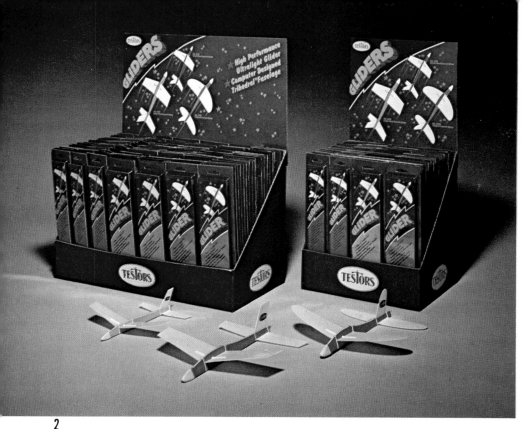

All gliders, no matter what their size, have one thing in common: they are engineless. The large, sophisticated ones such as the Olympic II from Cox (1), have wingspans of several feet and are equipped with servos that enable their pilots to control them from the ground using radio signals. These big gliders are often launched with a length of surgical tubing and nylon line. Cox makes a launching kit called the Launch Pail (3). Using such a system, a glider owner can send his craft hundreds of feet into the air. Other gliders called penny-planes are made of balsa wood or plastic. Testor makes several different models of plastic pennyplanes (2). They are launched with just a flick of the wrist.

2

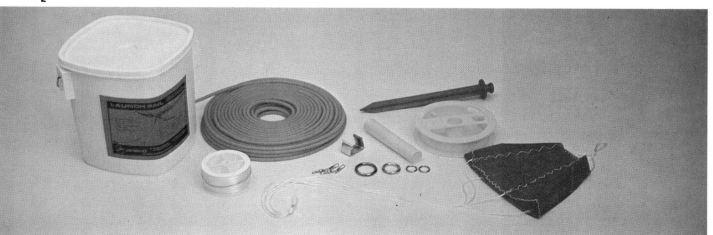

3

These are often made of intricate wooden skeletons covered with sheets of paper or plastic. Although the pieces may be precut and predrilled, great care must be taken at every step of assembly to ensure that the planes will perform well in flight. This becomes especially important when the movements of a ten-foot plane are controlled from the ground by expensive radio transmitters.

Once assembled, the more extravagant gliders are often given paint and decal treatment that is limited only by the talent and efforts of the builder.

Launching Methods

Pennyplanes are launched with just a flick of the wrist, or with a little rubber band on a stick. But when a glider has a wingspan of several feet, these launching systems may not be sufficient to get the plane into the air. Some gliders are launched by hand after the operators run with them across a field, but two other methods are more common.

The first is merely a larger version of the rubber band and stick. In this type of launch, a piece of surgical tubing (like that used for doctors' stethoscopes) perhaps 50 feet long is attached to a piece of nylon cord that is about 100 feet long. The tubing is anchored to a stake upwind, and the end of the cord is attached to the plane. A hook on the plane is designed to release the cord once the plane takes off. The user walks the plane back as far as 300 feet and then releases it. The resulting slingshot action can drive the plane to altitudes of 500 to 600 feet. The second launch method works with a winch. A motor-driven winding system takes up a length of cord that has been attached to the plane. This is similar to the system used by kite flyers as they pull in the string to make the kite climb. Launch systems like this can be found in most hobby shops or obtained from model dealers.

Once in the air, a glider's climb depends on its use of rising air currents, or thermals. In glider competition—and there is plenty of that available in AMA-sponsored national events and other, local get-togethers—success is measured in terms of how long a glider will remain aloft. This is affected by how well the glider uses those thermal air currents.

Gliders do not usually have any form of landing gear, as other airplanes do. Once the power that launches a glider is dissipated, gravity exerts its

1

2

Free-flight gliders—that is, gliders which are not controlled from the ground—include very large models (1) as well as the little pennyplanes that can be purchased in drugstores (4). Some gliders have wings made of single sheets of balsa (2), while others use balsa frameworks covered with a plastic skin. Many gliders with RC servos such as the Cadet from Cox (3) are available in kit form.

force to draw the airplane back to earth in a smooth and gentle glide. This path back to the ground is called the aircraft's glide path, and the glide path from its high point at the beginning of the glide to touchdown is called the radius of glide.

The glide path is also described in terms of its ratio of glide. This indicates the ratio between the altitude at which the glide began and the distance of the glide path to touchdown. If, for instance, the glide began at an altitude of 100 feet and continued a distance of 600 feet, the ratio of glide would be stated as 6:1.

Principles of Flight

The excitement of flying a glider comes from watching it utilize the air currents and soar for many minutes before making a graceful landing. The ratio of glide and the plane's ability to make the most of these currents is dependent upon the

3

4

builder's workmanship. That workmanship often is directly related to a good understanding of the principles of flight. Balance, stability, lift, thrust and drag are some of the terms used to describe how any type of aircraft behaves once it leaves the ground. All of these aspects of aerodynamics must be considered during construction of a large glider.

All planes are heavier than air. In order to fly, they must take advantage of the factors known as lift and thrust. Lift results from air passing over and under the wings and rear stabilizer. Since the top of an aircraft's wing is rounded, the air passing over the top travels farther and faster than the air passing under the wing. This results in less air pressure pushing down and more air pressure pushing up. The lift will remain in effect as long as the airplane is moving through the air. If the plane moves fast enough, the upward forces overcome the force of gravity and the craft remains airborne.

What moves an aircraft is called thrust. In a powered airplane, thrust is provided by the engine pushing or pulling it through the air. In a glider, thrust is generated by the original push or launch which set it in motion. As thrust and lift work to keep the airplane in flight, gravity and drag work against it. Drag is the friction of the air against the plane.

To keep your glider in flight as long as possible, you must maximize lift and thrust and minimize the effects of drag. These considerations must be kept in mind during the construction of the model as well as in flying it. The angle at which the wings meet the air, for example, is very important. The correct angle helps lift the airplane; too much tilt defeats the purpose.

Stability is another important factor. To be stable, an aircraft must be constructed so that it has a tendency to right itself when other forces act to put it out of balance. This tendency depends upon the aircraft's center of gravity. In model aviation, the center of gravity, or balance point, of an aircraft will vary depending on whether it is a free-flight model or one with a control line.

Good balance is particularly important when the aircraft model is brought in for a landing. If it is properly balanced, the plane should glide smoothly in for a landing; if not, it may take a nose dive that can be damaging to the plane and painful to its owner.

Careful construction and attention to detail are essential in building a successful model glider. A working understanding of basic aerodynamic principles is equally important. These factors grow in importance when you enter contests with your painstakingly constructed sailplane.

Among the competitive events for flyers of model gliders are time and distance contests involving every configuration of aircraft from the little penny-planes to the giant RC models. Information about these events is available from the Academy of Model Aeronautics.

Beginners in the hobby of flying radio-control gliders often select kits such as the Questor made by Cox (1). It has a wingspan of 62 inches. Gliders flown by more experienced modelers can be much bigger (2). The larger RC gliders contain more complex electronic gear, which makes them capable of a wider variety of maneuvers (3). All of them are silent and graceful in flight.

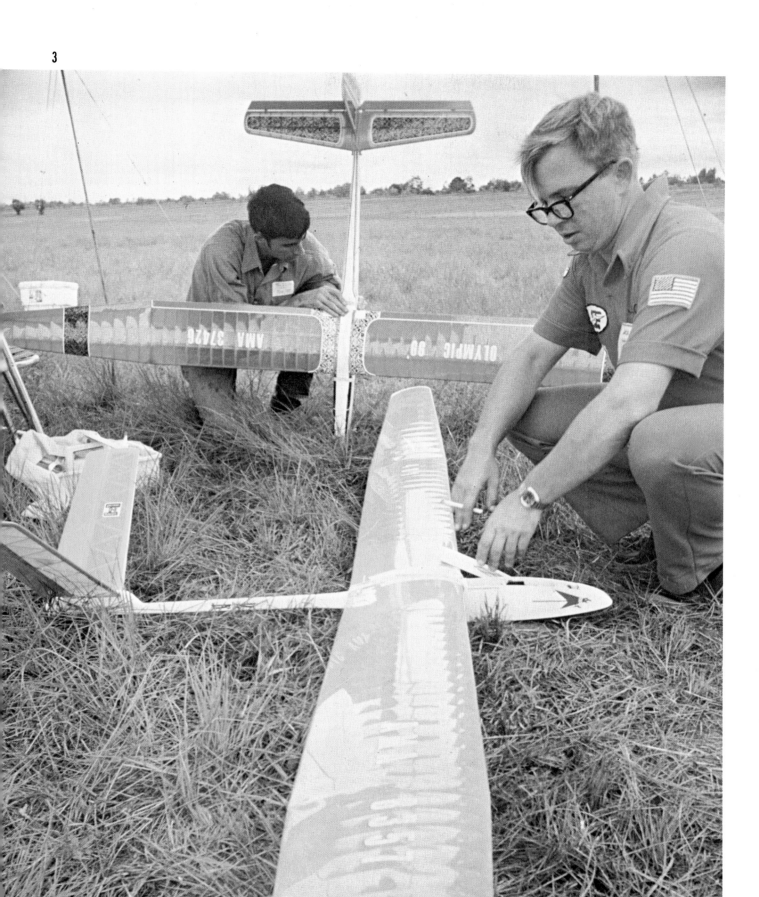

Rubber-Powered Models

1

SMALL PLASTIC SACKS full of balsa and plastic parts can still be purchased at toy and hobby stores for under a dollar. The pieces go together to form a plane that is little more than the most basic kind of glider, with the addition of a few extra pieces: a propeller, a long rubber band and perhaps some type of primitive landing gear. Assembly takes a few minutes, winding the rub-

ber-band "engine" takes a hundred or so turns of the propeller, and the plane takes off. The flight is short and the landing is often rocky, but there is a fascination in watching even this comical little plane fly across the backyard under its own power.

This is just the beginning of that fascination for many model airplane fans. As their interest in the hobby of flying rubber-powered aircraft grows, so

2

Rubber-powered models come in many different shapes and sizes. Some look like gliders (1), with very long wingspans. Others closely resemble real planes, such as early biplanes (2). Many of them do not attempt to look like a full-size plane, but instead are designed only for the longest possible flight (4). These larger rubber-powered planes require big rubber bands that often must be wound with a mechanical crank. Smaller ones (3) can be wound by hand, because their rubber "engines" are small. Some rubber-powered planes are launched by hand, while others are allowed to take off from runways just as full-size planes do.

3

4

does the complexity of the planes they build. The wood and other parts for more-advanced models are not expensive, but the amount of time spent in designing such planes from scratch or in decorating those built from kits can be great. As the hobbyist progresses, he or she may want to build models which closely resemble gasoline-powered models—some kits, in fact, come with instructions showing how either type of power can be used. Some of the larger rubber-powered planes have two or more engines. There is a wide range of types and sizes available.

Most of the kits for rubber-powered models provide only the basics. When beginning hobbyists first open a box, they may be surprised at just how little there appears to be in the kit: there are usually

1

a few diecut balsa parts; a propeller; "skin" for the body; decals; a rubber band; and instructions for assembly and, perhaps, for flying.

Special tissue paper, called rice paper, is the material most often used to cover the framework of rubber-powered model airplanes. This paper is light and tough—a matter of prime importance in the construction of these models. This type of tissue paper has a grain; that is, fibers running in a particular direction. The skin should be applied with the grain running parallel to the edges of the wings and lengthwise on the fuselage.

Model airplane dope, a thick lacquer, is generally considered the best material for applying the tissue

cover to the balsa frame. Once the tissue has been applied, it should be sprinkled with water and allowed to dry. This causes the paper to shrink and form a smooth, tight covering over the model aircraft frame.

A special type of ultralight rubber-powered model is flown only indoors. The propeller as well as the lifting surfaces of these model airplanes are covered with a special type of transparent film. It is about half as heavy as the tissue paper that is generally used for ordinary rubber-powered airplanes flown outdoors. It is so fragile that it will crumble if you touch it with your hands. This makes it somewhat difficult to use in construction. The

3

There is a great difference in the looks of rubber-powered planes that are meant to be flown outdoors and those designed to fly indoors. One outdoor plane is the Bristol Bullet (1) from Lee's Hobbies. The extremely light rubber-powered planes for indoor use (2, 3) do not have to be built to withstand gusts or wind, so they can be made of fragile frames and covered with very thin film.

2

material is formed by floating chemicals on water and allowing them to set, forming a film. The film is then applied to the frame either by using a wire hoop or by bringing the model's frame up through the water and into the film floating on the surface. The chemicals are available from hobby supply companies.

Flying Rubber-Powered Models

Rubber-powered models use wound-up rubber strips, sometimes called the "rubber motor," to provide thrust. The rubber strip is a type of rubber band that is specially made for use in model airplanes. These bands come in various widths depending on the size of the model. The thickness of the rubber bands used for these model planes is the same regardless of the band's width. It is most common to use rubber stripping much longer than the airplane and to loop it back and forth more than once from the hook on the propeller to the hook at the end of the fuselage. The rubber stripping is usually attached by lashing its ends to the hooks, allowing a little slack when it is installed.

Mechanical devices such as a hand drill, egg beater or a special model airplane winder can be used to wind the rubber motor of your airplane.

This is a much more convenient way to do it than to wind it by hand.

It is a good practice to break in a rubber motor by winding it perhaps 25 turns the first time, 50 the second time, and so on until its maximum elasticity is reached. Another good idea is to always have extra bands on hand. They are sold separately in hobby shops.

You will also need to lubricate the rubber stripping so that it can move smoothly and easily as it is wound and when it unwinds. You can buy a prepared lubricant from model airplane dealers or make your own by boiling shavings of hand soap (not detergents) in water and then mixing this thick solution with an equal amount of glycerin. Do not apply common oil or grease as a lubricant because this can rot the rubber. Be sure to apply the lubricant only on the wound part of the stripping and not on the ends that connect the rubber to the hooks: lubricant at the ends can cause the band to slip off.

If you plan to fly your rubber-powered airplane often, you will want to be sure to give proper care to the rubber motor so that it will last as long as possible. This includes protecting the rubber from sunlight, heat, oil or dust. Some hobbyists even wash and dry the rubber stripping after each use. Regardless of how much care you wish to give the motor, be sure to at least examine its condition before flight. If the rubber stripping should break during a flight, the airplane could be seriously damaged.

Other factors will determine how smooth the flight will be. One of them is balance. The more money and time you put into a rubber-powered model, the more care you will want to take to assure that it is balanced properly. Changes in the plane's weight and other mistakes during construction can throw it off balance. This can mean that every flight is followed by a repair job.

Modifications of the plane's propeller also can do harm. Fortunately, manufacturers of kits proportion the propellers to suit the planes. You may find that you want to experiment with different shapes or sizes of propellers, but the results can be damaging to the model.

Even after a smooth flight, your plane could be damaged when it lands. Some of the least expensive rubber-powered models have no landing gear at all, but the more refined ones have some sort of apparatus to reduce the impact of landing. This gear is generally a set of plastic wheels attached to the plane with springy wires that act as shock absorbers.

All of these factors are important in keeping your model in flying condition, and even more critical in competition. Numerous contests are held for builders of rubber-powered airplanes. They include indoor and outdoor distance flying and other events.

1

The rubber bands of the little rubber-powered planes sold in drugstores can be wound up with a finger. However, as the planes grow in size and the rubber bands become larger, special cranks are used to wind the lengths of rubber. These cranks can be held in the hand (2), but in some cases they are strapped to the user's shoulder with leather belts (1) to enable a maximum amount of muscle power to be put to work.

Engine-Powered Models

ENGINE-POWERED MODELS represent the highest level of sophistication and cost in the world of model aviation. While it is possible to buy small planes powered by motors that use CO_2 gas or simple electric motors to entertain a child, the upper limits of the hobby include truly mammoth models equipped with jet engines. Neither of these power sources is as common as the internal-combustion, or piston, engine.

These engines, which are scaled-down versions of powerplants used in automobiles and real planes, come in all sizes. Those used in the smallest planes can be bought for about $15, but others used in the largest models can cost upwards of $200 each. Some huge models use several of these powerful engines.

This category of flying models includes superbly maneuverable craft that are capable of performing intricate aerobatics. Contests for these planes involve obstacle courses, payload carrying, military maneuvers such as dive bombing and strafing, racing and high-altitude performance. The category includes more than planes: model helicopters that operate like full-size ones are also available. Engine-powered models can be controlled from the ground by wires held in the operator's hand, or by radio. These control systems can be used to adjust the model's speed, and to operate the wing flaps and stabilizer to change the plane's course.

Piston engines available for models today are highly efficient and technologically advanced. Many refinements in their design have been made over the years. These factors, combined with modern mass-production techniques, have brought hobbyists a wide selection of engines at reasonable prices. Cost can still be high enough to discourage modelers from owning several engines, but it is not necessary to have one for each model you wish to fly: the same engine can often be used for a number of different models.

As you first investigate the hobby of engine-powered models, you may want to buy a ready-made plane and use it to get the feel of controlling such a craft. Once you have progressed beyond that point and have become adept at building complex models, there are several points to consider when shopping for an engine. Some require a break-in period during which they must be operated on a bench mount before being used in a plane. Others are ready to be installed in the plane immediately. The only way to know if your engine should be broken in — or, for that matter, the proper type of fuel to use with it — is by carefully reading the directions that come with the engine.

Model airplane piston engines come in various sizes and therefore provide different amounts of power. The size of the engine is almost always expressed in terms of the displacement of the fuel/air mixture in cubic inches. The range is from .010 cubic inches up to .60 cubic inches, which can generate several horsepower. A model with a size of .19 means the fuel/air displacement is .19 cubic inches.

Types of Piston Engines

There are two basic types of miniature internal-combustion engines used with model airplanes

Many larger models use more than one engine.

today. By far the most common is the two-stroke engine. The other, considerably less common and usually more expensive, is the four-stroke type. Both have a piston which moves up and down within a cylinder. The piston is connected to the crankshaft, and, in turn, to the propeller.

The term "stroke" refers to the number of up or down movements of the piston and the connecting rod. In the common two-stroke engine, a cycle consists of a one-up, one-down motion to turn the

Radio-controlled stunt planes are small but powerful.

A flick of the prop starts the plane's engine.

crankshaft one revolution. In a four-stroke engine, the cycle consists of two up and down movements which result in two revolutions of the crankshaft for each cycle. In both cases, however, there is really only one actual "power" stroke for each cycle — the downward stroke caused by the burning of fuel. Two-stroke engines generally weigh less than four-stroke units do, cost less and are less complicated. Four-stroke engines operate more smoothly.

As you develop your model aviation skills, you may find yourself tinkering with your plane's en-gine, cleaning it and even modifying it. Therefore, let's take a closer look now at how typical engines work. The two strokes include one compression stroke and one firing stroke. A mixture of fuel and oil passes through the crankcase and enters below the cylinder. On the compression stroke, the piston rises. It closes the exhaust valve and the bypass valve, and compresses the fuel at the top of the cylinder. At the same time, new fuel enters the cylinder below. When the piston reaches the top, the fuel is ignited. This sends the piston downward in its power stroke. As the piston moves downward,

1

2

3

Manufacturers of model airplane engines also make mufflers to quiet the noisy little power-plants. Cox mufflers are rings with elliptical exhaust outlets (1). Another Cox engine has a spring starter that is used to spin the propeller and start the engine (2). Some muffler systems are not only functional, but add to the realistic appearance of the model (3). The engines used with model planes differ as to the type of flight desired. Some planes with long wingspans use relatively small engines for slow, graceful flights. Other planes that are smaller, like racing models (4), use engines that are large and powerful enough to set speed records.

the exhaust valve is opened, permitting the burned gas to escape. The downward stroke also partly compresses the fuel below the cylinder. Then, as the piston reaches the bottom of the cylinder, the bypass valve opens and allows the fuel to flow around the piston and into the top cylinder. Then the cycle begins again.

In a four-stroke engine, the fuel enters and remains above the piston. On the first stroke, the piston moves downward; as it does, fuel is admitted into the cylinder from above. When the piston has reached the bottom of the cylinder, the intake valve

4

closes and the piston moves upward in its second stroke compressing the fuel vapors. When the piston reaches the end of its upward stroke, the fuel is ignited and explodes. This sends the piston downward, producing the third, or power, stroke. As the piston reaches the bottom, the exhaust valve opens to allow the burned gas to escape. As the piston rises again, it pushes the exhaust out of the cylinder with the fourth stroke.

Most model airplane engines have only one cylinder. Some, however, have been built with two or four. More cylinders develop more power, but add to the plane's weight.

Fuel and Air

How well an engine works depends greatly on how well it compresses fuel. Most model plane engines today use a mixture of methanol (a type of alcohol) as the primary fuel, and a synthetic oil or castor oil as a lubricant. Diesel engines use a mixture of kerosene, ether and oil.

The oil mixed with the fuel in engines lubricates the cylinder and serves as a seal between the piston and the cylinder wall. When a piston wears out and no longer fits a cylinder tightly, the engine's ability to compress fuel is greatly reduced. This reduces engine efficiency and power.

The compression ratio of any engine is the ratio between the volume of the fuel when the piston is at the bottom of the cylinder (when fuel has just entered the cylinder) and volume when the piston is as close to the top as it can be and the fuel is compressed. If this compressed fuel occupies a space that is one-sixth the space occupied before the fuel was compressed, the ratio is expressed as 6:1.

Sometimes a two-stroke engine will fire only on every other compression stroke. This condition, often called "four-cycling," results when more fuel enters the cylinder than can be properly compressed. The unexploded fuel passes through the exhaust on the power stroke. The result is that the engine fires at the end of the next compression stroke and the engine no longer runs smoothly.

Another factor that determines how well an engine runs is the mixture of air and fuel. Combining air with vaporized fuel is called carburetion. Model aircraft carburetion is controlled by a needle valve on the fuel tube. Air is sucked into the engine through the air intake. The fuel enters through a fuel line at a right angle and the fuel tube opens at the center. The needle enters this opening. By adjusting the regulating screw or handle on the outside, the needle can be moved in or out of the fuel tube. This adjusts the amount of fuel released.

If there is a high ratio of fuel to air, it is described as a rich mixture; a low ratio of fuel to air is called lean. It is important to keep in mind that fuel mixtures tend to become leaner in flight than when the aircraft is on the ground. For this reason, it is best

1

to find the proper setting on the ground and then slightly withdraw the needle to compensate for the difference in flight.

Starting the Engine

Early internal-combustion engines for model planes were generally ignited by a spark. These types of engines are still used by a few modelers, but by far the more popular types today are the glow plug and glow head types. Some diesel engines are also used.

Glow plug and glow head ignition are much the same, with the primary difference being that a glow plug is screwed into a cylinder head while a glow head is built onto the cylinder head. In the latter, therefore, the complete head must be replaced if a new firing element is needed. Glow plug or glow head ignitions are much simpler than spark plug ignitions. Spark plugs require additional attachments including a timing device, an ignition coil, condenser, battery and wiring—all of which would add weight to the model. Glow plugs call for only an engine and a fuel tank.

With a glow plug or glow head ignition engine, a battery is used to heat the firing element for the first explosion; once the engine is running, the battery is disconnected. The battery is required only to start the engine; from then on the explosions of the fuel will keep it sufficiently hot. The battery used for this purpose is a dry-cell ignition battery that can be purchased at any hobby shop. Wires are run from each terminal of the battery: one wire connects to the insulated post on top of the glow plug,

2

3

At any meet of hobbyists who fly engine-powered model planes, you can see people syphoning fuel from cans into squeeze bottles and then squirting it into the small tanks in the planes (1). Others will be connecting the electrical wires to the glow plugs of their planes' engines (2). Other pilots will be conferring with organizers (3) as they prepare to send their aircraft down the runway for what they hope will be a prize-winning flight.

and the other wire connects to the uninsulated cylinder head.

Diesel engines do not have a separate ignition element. This is because the fuel they use explodes when compressed in the cylinder. To start a diesel engine on an aircraft model, you just turn the propeller. This begins the compression and power cycle. Compression of the vapors releases heat, and the engine continues to fire itself.

Most diesel engines have variable compression, which means that the compression can be adjusted by moving a lever. The engine is usually started at a high compression rate and then lowered once the engine is running smoothly. Diesel engines are generally built to work at a higher compression ratio than glow plug engines. Many modelers, however, think diesel engines are less reliable for start-

ing than glow plug engines. Diesel engines do require an adjustment of both a needle valve which controls the fuel/air mixture and an adjustment of the compression ratio. Glow plug engines require adjustment of only the needle valve.

Whichever type of engine you use, proper care of it will have a major effect on how long it will last. When it is not in use, keep the engine wrapped in a cloth so that it will not collect dust. When you must remove plugs or cylinder heads, be sure to use wrenches made especially for this purpose. They are available at most hobby shops or from mail-order dealers. Use of pliers or ordinary wrenches can often result in damage to your engine. Also be sure you never force or overtighten any part of the engine. With adequate care, a model engine can provide many hours of flight time.

Control-Line Flying

1

CONTROL-LINE FLYING allows the hobbyist to take an active role in the flight of model aircraft. It can be a starting point for novices, because many models are available that are simple in design and ready to fly the moment they come out of the box. It can also be a major step in expert modelers' progress through the hobby of model aviation as they engineer and assemble their own high-performance craft.

There are essentially two types of ''line'' flying. In the first type, one end of a line or cord is fastened to an engine-powered plane and the other end is secured to a post or held in the operator's hand. This does not give the user great control over the plane, but it does allow the model to be observed closely as it flies in a large circle. In the second type, several lines can be run from a hand-held unit to mechanical connections in the plane. This sys-

2

3

tem enables the operator to make changes in the model's speed, altitude and direction. The first type is called tethered flying; the second is called U-control or control-line flying.

There is another kind of control-line flying that is really just a combination of the other two. Model airplanes having internal combustion engines and a wingspan of 24 inches or less are sometimes flown from a center post, but these models use two lines and what turns out to be an automatic-pilot device. The two lines are set up as they would be for an actual control-line flight, but they are attached to a swivel post. The automatic piloting results because the model's elevators (altitude controls) are set in a neutral position at a level even with the top of the post. When the airplane begins to move above this position, the elevators automatically react to bring it back down to the position that is level with the top of the post; when it moves below that position, the elevator will again adjust, this time to bring it back up. This form of tethered flying is becoming increasingly popular because it requires only one person to handle the entire take-off, flight and landing operation. Another advantage is that it requires a much smaller area than what would be needed for other control-line flights. An area where the plane can circle only 15 feet from the post is usually sufficient for this type of tethered flying.

Early types of control-line model aircraft involved a cable that carried current to the airplane's electric motor from a battery on the ground. More effective for the hobbyist today, however, are rubber-powered and internal-combustion (or sometimes jet) engines that locate the complete power source within the airplane. Only the control device remains on the ground.

The control system usually consists of two lines running from the hand-held control panel to the model. They move the elevators using a mechanism called a bellcrank inside the plane. These lines, usually anywhere from 25 to 70 feet long, work mechanically rather than electrically. Occasionally, another function is added: a third line controls the speed of the engine. On advanced models, it may also operate additional wing flaps called ailerons which control the plane's side-to-side rolling motion. This third line can operate either mechanically or electrically.

Models or kits do not, in most cases, come with the U-control apparatus, but everything you will need is available from hobby shops and model airplane dealers.

Flying Control-Line Models

Small, rubber-powered aircraft usually need nothing more than string as a tether; but for engine-powered models, a much stronger line must be used. The proper material will depend on the size of the model and the expected range of its flight. It can be anything from fishing line to steel wire or cable. Hobby shop personnel should be able to help you in picking the right tether.

There are certain considerations and safety precautions which apply to both tethered and control-line models. First, be sure to periodically check the line for any frayed or defective areas. If you find any, replace or repair them immediately so the line will not break and cause damage to your airplane or injure someone in the area. A fast-moving plane with a sharp propeller can become a frightening hazard if it is not carefully controlled and responsibly looked after. Always be certain that you are a safe distance away from spectators, and be careful to avoid electrical cables. You could be electrocuted if your aircraft or its lines become tangled in electrical wires.

1

2

Manufacturers of control-line planes make a number of models for beginners. Cox makes the F-15 Falcon (1, top) and the Hustler (1, bottom) for youngsters. They have blunt-edged propellers for safety. Two other Cox models for novices,` the Piper Commanche (2, top) and the Skymaster (2, bottom) feature automatic pilot. This system makes automatic adjustments to keep the plane on a level course. Once a beginner has logged many hours of control-line flight time with one of the simpler planes, he or she may want to move up to speed models (3). These planes are not built to resemble real aircraft, but instead are designed for top speed. They use powerful engines and a streamlined shape to cut wind resistance (4).

3

4

Both tether cords and control lines produce a drag effect on model airplanes. To offset this drag, all airplanes flown with lines must be adjusted to bring them into balance. One method is to weight down the wing on the side opposite the line. Another is to increase the lifting area of the wing nearest the cable. You may have to use a combination of these methods to achieve proper balance.

It is important that the control lines between the airplane and the pilot on the ground be kept taut at all times. Otherwise, you will lose control of the plane. Centripetal force as well as the balance and design of the airplane will help promote this, but it is still the responsibility and skill of the pilot which determine the success of the flight. Learning to fly a model airplane by control line takes a good amount of practice and experiment. The beginner will usually tend to overdo the basic movements: only a slight movement is necessary for normal control. The airplane model used will make a considerable difference, because some are much less responsive than others. Another factor to keep in mind is that the distance between the lines on the control handle will affect the amount of control. The farther apart they are, the greater the pull sent to the plane from the control panel.

Planes to Fly

It is probably wise for the control-line beginner to obtain initial experience flying a "trainer" airplane. Trainer kits are readily available from most hobby

1

shops. They can provide valuable flying experience and practice—factors that contribute to proficiency in control-line flying. Trainers are often the first models used by novices because they are comparatively unresponsive and slow. This is an advantage when you are first learning to fly because these models will compensate for the beginner's inclination to give too much control. Trainers are usually made of molded plastic or wooden components, or a combination of both.

The next step up brings you to the sport models. They are beyond the basic trainers in ability. They, too, are available ready-made or in kits.

Control-line scale model airplanes move the user into the arena of the advanced modeler. They come as wood or plastic kits or are made from scratch by following specific plans. Scale models can be very elaborate, and there is a wide variety to choose from.

Speed models are streamlined aircraft, highly sensitive to control. They are built for speed, not maneuverability. These are the models that set speed records. Speed models seldom have landing gear; they usually take off from a dolly which is left behind and then land on a metal skid, often called a speed pan, attached to their underside.

Take-off and Landing

Other types of models have landing gear that closely resembles that of full-size planes. As only experience can illustrate, there is a knack to success-

2

Most control-line planes use internal-combustion engines, but some of them use other types of motors. Two fuel-powered planes from Cox that are designed for beginners are the Mantis (1, top) and the F-15 Eagle (1, bottom). An intermediate model from Cox is the Super Sport Trainer (4). Intermediate models provide more of a challenge to their pilots. For very young children who are not ready for fuel-powered planes, Cox makes several battery-powered models, including the Spitfire (3, top) and the Fireball (3, bottom). Expert control-line pilots often spend many weeks building models that are nearly exact duplicates of the full-size planes (2).

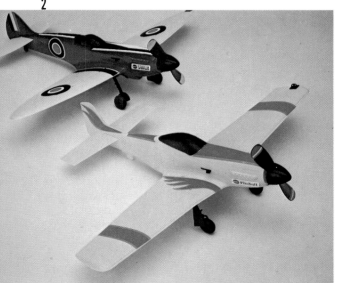

3

4

Ready-to-fly planes for the advanced control-line pilot are available from several companies. Cox makes the JU-87D Stuka (1, top) and Combat Mustang (1, bottom) for hobbyists who have had a lot of experience in flying control-line planes. For even more advanced control-line fliers, plans are available for the construction of much larger planes (2). They are challenging enough to test the assembly and flying skills of the most experienced control-line enthusiast. Other advanced control-line pilots concentrate their efforts on building models that are small but very fast (3). The ground control systems for these planes are complex.

1

2

ful take-offs and landings.

Control-line models are not launched into the wind: they must be launched with the wind behind them so that they can attain enough speed to counter the effect of crosswinds. If you are a control-line beginner, start with a fairly short line—maybe only about 25 feet long—and do not fly your plane if the wind is too strong.

Take-off works best from a hard, flat surface; but landing is safest on a soft, grassy area. Bringing a control-line aircraft in for a safe landing is difficult

for a beginner and faulty landings can damage your model. It is often wise to gain your experience at landing models having flexible plastic propellers.

Once you have acquired some experience in the basics of take-offs, flight and landings, you may want to enter your plane in contests for control-line hobbyists. There are many organized competitions, both on the national and international level and in local club contests.

One colorful event which has become quite popular recently is the aircraft carrier contest. Models

3

must take off from and then land on a model of an aircraft carrier. The pilot's skill at take-off, high-speed and low-speed maneuvering, and landing are all evaluated. Any model airplane with a wingspan up to 44 inches can be used.

Combat competitions are also held with control-line planes. Paper streamers are attached to the aircraft and the object is to use your propeller to slash your opponent's streamers. Model airplanes used for this type of event must be highly maneuverable and fast. Stunt flying is another category of competition. These models, too, must be very maneuverable. They must also be able to fly in any position, even upside down. There are many different competitive events for stunt model airplanes: some suggested by the Academy of Model Aeronautics; others from the wild imaginations of experienced model pilots.

Speed races are also a common competition with control-line models. Races that involve refueling and other ground maintenance can test the skill not only of the pilot but the ground crew as well.

Radio-Control Flying

1

RADIO CONTROL truly puts the model aviator in the driver's seat, even though that seat stays on the ground. It is not just simulated piloting, but real piloting in every sense of the word. With no lines to hold the plane on course, the operator of the RC unit must make subtle corrections in the aircraft's direction by sending out electronic sig- nals over radio waves. It begins as a struggle to keep the plane from crashing, and progresses to the point where astoundingly intricate feats of aerobatics are possible.

These radio-control units work with engine- powered craft of all sorts, including planes and helicopters. They also work with gliders, allowing

2

A major part of radio-controlled model airplane flying is the piloting of RC gliders. Some of these engineless planes are launched by hand (1, 4). Others are pulled into the air with tow-lines or long lengths of surgical tubing (3). One such RC glider, the Super Questor (2) is manufactured by Cox. These planes respond to radio signals by changing the position of their rudders, stabilizers and ailerons. In this way, the ground pilot can maneuver the plane to make optimum use of air currents to climb, dive, circle and come to a graceful landing.

3

4

the pilot to make the most of air currents and thermals.

In many cases, the RC system is purchased as a separate item for use with a plane kit, and the electronic components are installed in the plane by the builder. However, there are models available which include the hand-held control panel and the electric components already in place in the plane. These models are ideal for the hobbyist who is more interested in flying planes than in building them.

Whether the RC unit is purchased with the plane or separately, it will be similar in design to all others. The RC system will consist of control panel, battery pack, plane-mounted components called servos, frequency flag (to tell other RC pilots which wavelength you are using) and an instruction booklet. The equipment is available in a broad range of complexity and at prices from about $60 to well over $500. The simplest units perform one basic function, while the most sophisticated ones include controls for a number of operations.

The single function of the most elementary kind of unit determines the position of the plane's rudder. The rudder can be used to steer the plane to the right and left. However, because of the design of planes having only this function, the RC operator can also control the craft's altitude by manipulating the rudder. That is because a properly designed RC model will climb when the rudder is in a neutral position; but when the rudder is moved to the right or left, the plane will bank and turn. If the rudder is held in the right or left position, the aircraft will descend in a circular path.

If radio control of the model should be lost because of battery failure, the rudder usually slips into neutral and the plane climbs and flies away. It may not stop until it runs out of fuel, often far from the pilot. For this reason, some of the more elaborate RC planes have fail-safe systems that bring the model gently down to earth when radio control is lost.

Novices often find the rudder-only control system to be exciting and challenging. But after pilots have developed the skills to effectively control the plane's rudder, they may want to move on to RC systems with other functions. These advanced systems add elevator and aileron controls, throttle adjustments and battery voltage meters to the rudder control. The elevator controls offer a more direct means of adjusting the plane's altitude. The ailerons control the plane's roll, allowing the wings to rotate end over end.

Whether an engine-powered plane is equipped with rudder adjustments only or with a number of controls, it must have an engine and fuel system that will operate when the plane flies nose-up, nose-down and even during rolls and somersaults. The system must be able to feed fuel to the engine in all flight positions. To that end, some RC planes have pressurized fuel tanks to assure adequate supply of fuel at all times.

How RC Works

It is a good idea for any serious modeler or prospective modeler to have a sound working knowl-

1

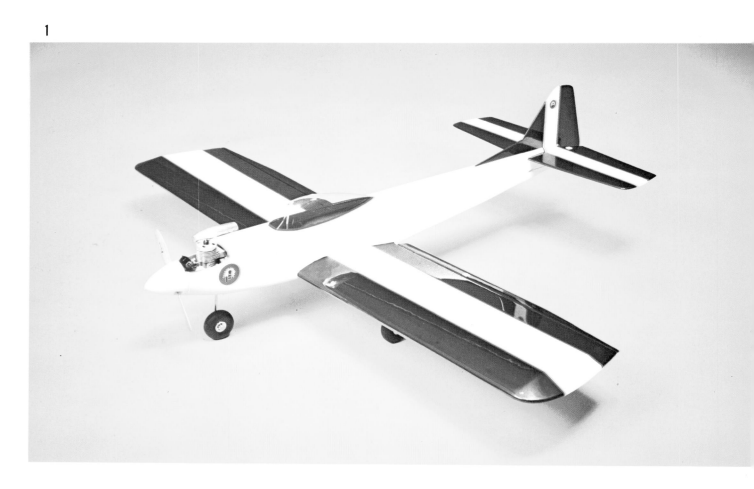

2

3

4

The New Era, an engine-powered RC plane from Cox (1), is equipped with electronic servos that permit it to perform a wide variety of stunts during flights of up to ten minutes. A Cox model for the novice radio-control pilot is the Q-Tee (4). Many RC hobbyists are as much concerned with the appearance of their plane as they are with the model's performance in the air, and spend many hours creating models which closely resemble full-size planes (2). With their RC panels in hand, model airplane pilots can truly get the feel of controlling every movement of the aircraft, from takeoff (3) to landing.

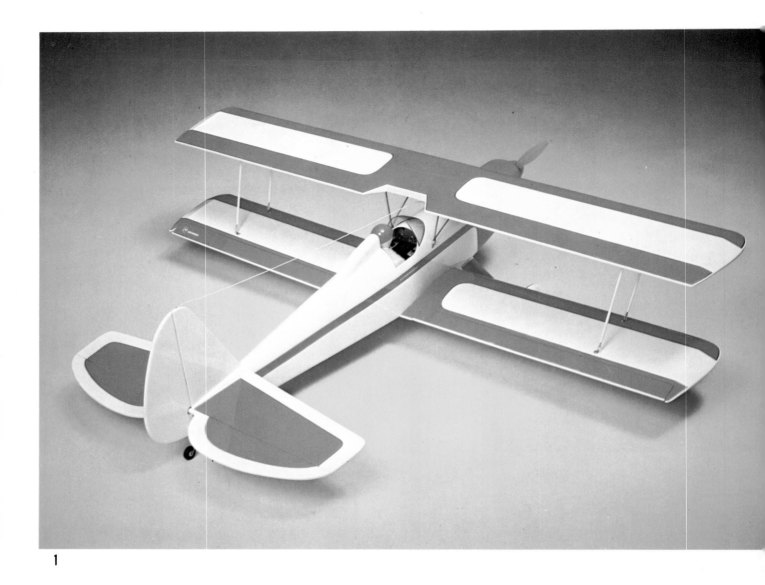

1

edge of how radio remote control operates. Here is a very brief and simplified explanation.

The transmitter in the hands of the pilot sends out a radio signal by way of the RC antenna. The receiver in the model airplane is tuned to the transmitter's frequency. The signal is picked up by the airplane's antenna. The most common method of transmission today in model aviation is with tone-modulated waves. A signal is continuously transmitted once the transmitter is switched on. The receiver on the airplane picks up the signal, but no function is performed until the pilot manipulates a control on the transmitter. This imposes a tone on the radio wave, and the receiver in the aircraft picks this up as a command.

Earlier receivers that used tubes, rather than transistors, were not able to pick up enough energy to actually perform the desired function. The energy received was used to operate a relay switch that activated batteries to perform the control function. This type of receiver is called a relay receiver.

The trend today, however, is toward receivers that use transistors, and they can operate the control function directly. The action that results from the radio-control direction is a mechanical movement which is activated through the servos on the model aircraft.

Not too many years ago, it was necessary to pass an extensive test to obtain a radio license before you could fly a model airplane. There is no longer a test requirement, but a license from the Federal Communications Commission is necessary. The reason is that when you are flying a model airplane by remote control, you are in effect operating a small radio station. To obtain a license, you must send the proper form to the FCC.

Once you have your license and have become adept at flying an RC model, you may want to enter contests held frequently by organizations of RC enthusiasts. The competition includes such events as pylon racing, pattern maneuvers, speed racing and cargo carrying.

The Cox Acro Star (1) is a radio-control biplane that can perform an unlimited variety of stunts, provided that the pilot knows exactly what he or she is doing. Larger, even more complex RC models are flown for speed as well as acrobatics (2). The control panels that enable these planes to do their tricks are available in different levels of complexity. Cox/Sanwa makes several units. The model 8020 (3) is a two-channel system, designed for use by youngsters and other beginning RC hobbyists. A more sophisticated RC unit, the model 8060 (4), can transmit instructions to a plane on six channels, enabling the pilot to put his plane through a greater number of movements.

2

3

4

Sources

Associations and Organizations

THE FOLLOWING are some of the associations serving the model aviation world; each offers specific and specialized benefits to the modeler. In addition, we have listed some of the important national and international agencies which also provide helpful information.

Academy of Model Aeronautics
815 15th Street, N.W.
Washington, DC 20005
   This non-profit, educational association is the governing body for flying-model aviation in the United States. The AMA is a division of the National Aeronautic Association and is recognized by the Federation Aeronautique Internationale, the world governing body for all aviation activities. The AMA currently has more than 60,000 members and sponsors over 1300 model aviation clubs throughout the United States. The AMA offers a wide variety of services including a monthly magazine, a monthly calendar of all model aviation competitions, a youth scholarship program and sponsorship of air show teams. It serves as a general clearinghouse for information about model aviation on a national and local scale. The AMA sponsors more than 1000 competitions each year, each with more than 90 different events. It also provides a liaison between the modeler and the Federal Aviation Adminis-

tration and the Federal Communications Commission. The AMA is open to anyone interested in model aircraft that fly.

Federal Aviation Administration
800 Independence Ave., S.W.
Washington, DC 20591
The FAA is the government agency that regulates and licenses all aviation activities in the United States.

Federal Communications Commission
1919 M Street, N.W.
Washington, DC 20554
This government agency regulates and licenses all radio equipment operators in the United States. Applications for a Citizens Radio Service license, required for operation of RC models, are sent to the FCC.

CL Racing Pilots & Mechanics Association
c/o Russ Sandusky
1122 Plaza Circle
Joppa, MD 21085
This organization for model racers and crew covers all aspects of model aircraft racing, publicizing contests, developing procedural rules and regulations and keeping records.

FAI Control Line Society
c/o Laird Jackson
523 Meadowbrook Circle
St. Davids, PA 19087
Geared to represent all aspects of control line competition, this group provides information on various contests.

International Miniature Aerobatics Club
c/o Eric Clapp
16970 Barnell Ave.
Morgan Hill, CA 95037
This is the organization for devotees of miniatures that fly and compete.

International Plastic Modelers Society/USA
P. O. Box 2555
Long Beach, CA 90801
IPMS/USA is the largest organization for static model builders in the United States. It is a non-profit, educational organization geared to improving the art and craft of plastic modeling. IPMS/USA offers membership to anyone interested in the hobby and provides a variety of helpful services including: sponsoring chapters throughout the country; providing guidelines, rules and sponsorship of competitions and contests; distributing specialized publications; and holding a national convention each year for static modeling enthusiasts. Present membership is about 5000 in the United States. .

League of Silent Flight
P.O. Box 39068
Chicago, IL 60639
The interest here is in RC soaring (gliders). This is an international organization where membership must be earned.

Miniature Aircraft Combat Association
c/o Patty Sasnett
1443 McKinley Ave.
Escondido, CA 92027
For the control-line combat enthusiast, this organization helps organize and operate contests and define rules and procedures.

Model Engine Collectors Association
c/o Hank Hilscher
P.O. Box 725
Indianapolis, IN 46206
This organization is both a focal point and clearinghouse for information about antique, scale and miniature models. It provides guides, tips and classified ads for engines and other parts.

National Aeronautic Association
821 15th Street, N.W.
Washington, DC 20005
This organization supervises all sporting aviation competition in the United States for both full-size and model aircraft. NAA is the official overseer of all aeronautic records in the United States.

National Free Flight Society
c/o Doug Galbreath
707 Second St.
Davis, CA 95616
As its name implies, this is the organization for the free-flight enthusiast.

National Indoor Model Airplane Society
P.O. Box 545
Richardson, TX 75080
This is the national headquarters for indoor model flying; national and international activites and competitions are covered.

National Miniature Pylon Racing Association
c/o Whit Stockwell
4000 Hayvenhurst Ave.
Encino, CA 91436
This is considered the chief organization for the flying and competing of RC miniature aircraft.

National Radio Control Helicopter Association
c/o R/C Modeler Magazine
P.O. Box 487
Sierra Madre, CA 91024
Under the auspices of one of the most prestigious publications in the RC field, this organization

promotes and coordinates all aspects of model helicopter operation.

National Society of Radio Controlled Aerobatics
c/o Sally Brown
8534 Huddleston Drive
Cincinnati, OH 45236

This organization caters to the aerobatic modeler and competitor. It is active in competition, rules and procedures.

Precision Aerobatics Model Pilots Association
c/o Wynn Paul
1640 Maywick Drive
Lexington, KY 40504

Stunt flying and control-line precision aviation is the emphasis of this organization.

Society of Antique Modelers
1947 Superior Ave.
Whiting, IN 46394

This is a respected organization devoted to promoting, coordinating and developing activities related to models of antique and historic aircraft, including free-flight and RC models.

Women Inter-National Glider Soaring
c/o Karen Toebe
6128 Marscot St.
Lansing, MI 48910

Specifically devoted to women with an interest in glider soaring, this organization covers both the basic hobby of soaring as well as all related competitions.

Publications

Periodicals

THE FOLLOWING are some of the leading publications today in the field of model aviation. They offer a broad range of advice, information and news of current events for the model airplane builder and flier.

Flying Models, P.O. Box 700, Newton, NJ 07860. Started back in 1928 as Flying Aces, this magazine has long been a respected one in the field of model aviation. Today, its emphasis is on radio-control models, but it also occasionally includes control-line and other model aviation subjects. Published monthly, it contains good articles and product information and reviews.

IPMS/USA Quarterly, International Plastic Model Society, P.O. Box 2555, Long Beach, CA 90801. This official publication of IPMS/USA contains a good selection of in-depth articles on various facets of static models. Published four times a year, it comes with membership in IPMS/USA.

Model Airplane News, Air Age Inc., 1 North Broadway, White Plains, NY 10601. This monthly magazine has been around since 1929, providing informative articles on all facets of model airplaning — from static model building to RC competition winners. It is a good source for up-to-date products and new models. Available by subscription and on newsstands.

Model Aviation, Academy of Model Aeronautics, 815 15th St., N.W., Washington, DC 20005. This is the official publication of the AMA, published monthly. A subscription is included as part of a membership in AMA. It is informative and current in its reporting on the world of model aviation. It includes a comprehensive calendar of events, covering all competitions, meetings and special events throughout the United States.

Model Builder, 621 W. 19th St., Costa Mesa, CA 92627. This monthly magazine presents informative articles and detailed building plans for a wide variety of flying models. It contains in-depth material for the serious modeler and model aviator. Available by subscription and on the newsstand.

Radio Control Buyers Guide, Boynton & Associates, Clifton House, Clifton, VA 22024. This helpful publication provides information about more than 2000 RC products: systems, accessories and manufacturers. It can be a big help to the serious RC modeler.

RC Modeler, 120 W. Sierra Madre Blvd., Sierra Madre, CA 91024. The largest and most thorough of the monthly magazines in its coverage, this publication contains a wealth of specialized articles about the hobby as well as the latest in equipment and models for the RC enthusiast. It is highly respected and provides a broad range of services to the reader as well as pertinent and timely information. Available by subscription or on newsstands.

RC Sportsman, P.O. Box 11247, Reno, NV 89520. Published monthly, this tabloid color newspaper reaches a large number of RC enthusiasts throughout the country. It provides a good range of topical articles as well as detailed plans for some unique models and information about products.

Scale Aircraft Modeler, Challenge Publications, Inc., 7950 Deering Ave., Canoga Park, CA 91304. This is a magazine for the static model airplane maker, complete with informative articles, detailed construction plans and plenty of tips. Each quarterly issue presents a diverse selection of static models with good full-color illustrations. Available by subscription or on newsstands.

Scale Modeler, Challenge Publications Inc., 7950 Deering Ave., Canoga Park, CA 91304. This is the most popular and widely read magazine in the field of static model building. Published monthly, it provides informative articles on many types of models. Tips, hints and plenty of full-color photographs add to its val-

ue. Available by subscription or on the newsstand.

Scale R/C Modeler, Challenge Publications, Inc., 7950 Deering Ave., Canoga Park, CA 91304. A specialized magazine directed to the RC scale-model enthusiast, it can be helpful to other serious aviation modelers as well. It includes informative articles about the models and those who have created them as well as plans, tips and good full-color illustrations. Published bimonthly, it is available by subscription or on the newsstand.

Update, International Plastic Model Society, P.O. Box 2555, Long Beach, CA 90801. This is the official magazine/newsletter of IPMS/USA and is published six times a year. Averaging 24 pages an issue, it is full of modeling tips, techniques and "how-to" articles as well as coverage of contests and general goings-on in the field of static plastic modeling. A subscription comes with membership in IPMS/USA.

Books

Hundreds of books on airplanes, aviation, the science of aeronautics and other related subjects are available. In addition, there are many specialized booklets for the model airplane builder, flier and competitor from tips on airbrushing to detailed flight training.

One source for books, of course, is your local library. If you want to own some, however, you can find them in bookstores, hobby shops, model airplane specialty stores or through the mail-order houses that serve the model aviation world. Here are two other sources.

AMA Rule Book, Academy of Model Aeronautics, 815 15th St., N.W., Washington, DC 20005. A complete guide to sport and competitive model aviation, the rule book is an official publication of the AMA and as comprehensive a book (100 pages) as you can find on the subject. It includes rules, procedures and guides for setting up and conducting competitive events and is updated each year.

R/C Modeler Magazine Books, 120 W. Sierra Madre Blvd., Sierra Madre, CA 91024. The respected R/C Modeler Company publishes a number of specialized and very helpful books for the RC hobbyist from general overview to the specifics of scale, engines, wings and flight training.

Manufacturers & Distributors

BASIC SOURCES for model airplanes and accessories are hobby shops in your area and mail-order companies specializing in model aircraft supplies. The following list of manufacturers and distributors may help you as you investigate the hobby. In many cases, the firms listed here supply catalogs, how-to booklets and other materials that can be of great help to modelers. You may want to write to them to obtain some of these publications and get an overview of what types of products are available.

STATIC AIRPLANE MODELS AND DIORAMAS

Airtec
128 South Rd.
Enfield, CT 06082

AMT
Lesney AMT Corp.
3031 James St.
Baltimore, MD 21230

Bachman
1400 Erie Ave.
Philadelphia, PA 19124

Entex Industries
1100 W. Walnut St.
Compton, CA 90220

Guillow's
40 New Salem St.
Wakefield, MA 01880

J & L Aircraft Models
P. O. Box 6004
Torrance, CA 90504

Krasel Industries, Inc.
1821 E. Newport Circle
Santa Ana, CA 92705

Minicraft/Hasegawa
1510 W. 228th St.
Torrance, CA 90501

Monogram Models
8601 Waukegan Rd.
Morton Grove, IL 60053

Otaki (See Scale Craft)

Revell Inc.
4223 Glencoe Ave.
Venice, CA 90291

Scale Craft Models, Inc.
8735 Shirley Ave.
Northridge, CA 91324

Tamiya
Model Rectifier Corp.
2500 Woodbridge Ave.
Edison, NJ 08817

ASSEMBLY MATERIALS, TOOLS AND ACCESSORIES

Armtec
128 South Rd.
Enfield, CT 06082

Astro-Flight Inc.
13377 Beach Ave.
Venice, CA 90291

Baca Products
19 Hawthorne Lane
Streamwood, IL 60103

Badger Air-Brush Co.
9128 W. Belmont Ave.
Franklin Park, IL 60131

Balsa USA
P.O. Box 164
Marinette, WI 54143

B & D Enterprises
P.O. Box 2268, Pike Station
Rockville, MD 20852

Brice Machine Specialties
14722 Leahy Ave.
Bellflower, CA 90706

BWT Systems
161 Anita Drive
Pickerington, OH 43147

Carmel Industries Inc.
50-20 25th St.
Long Island City, NY 11101

Custom Craft Products
19 Florgate Rd.
Farmingdale, NY 11735

DA Enterprises
P.O. Box 335
Haubstadt, IN 47639

Dremel Manufacturing
4915 21st St.
Racine, WI 53406

EMG Engineering Co.
18518 S. Broadway
Gardena, CA 90248

F.A.I. Model Supply
P.O. Box 9778
Phoenix, AZ 85068

Fox Manufacturing Co.
5305 Towson Ave.
Fort Smith, AR 72901

Fusite
Division, Emerson Electric Co.
6000 Fernview Ave.
Cincinnati, OH 45212

Grabber
P.O. Box 337
Hwy 56 West
Edgerton, KS 66021

Hobbypoxy
36 Pine St.
Rockaway, NJ 07866

Jim Crocket
1442 N. Fruit Ave.
Fresno, CA 93728

K & B Manufacturing
12152 Woodruff Ave.
Downey, CA 90241

K & S Engineering
6917 W. 59th St.
Chicago, IL 60638

Model Builder Products
621 W. 19th St.
Costa Mesa, CA 92627

Paasche Airbrush Co.
1909 W. Diversey Parkway
Chicago, IL 60614

Pactra Industries, Inc.
7060 Hollywood Blvd.
Los Angeles, CA 90028

Perry Aeromotive Inc.
581 N. Twin Oaks Valley Rd.
San Manos, CA 92069

Prather Products
1660 Ravenna Ave.
Wilmington, CA 96744

Progress Manufacturing Co.
P. O. Box 912
Manhattan, KS 66052

Robart Manufacturing Co.
P.O. Box 122
Wheaton, IL 60187

Royal Products Corp.
790 W. Tennessee
Denver, CO 80223

Sonic Tronics, Inc.
518 Ryers Ave.
Cheltenham, PA 19012

Space Age Fuels
  Route 3
  Kewanee, IL 61443
Sullivan Products Inc.
  535 Davisville Rd.
  Willow Grove, PA 19090
Su-Pr-Line Products
  Plainfield, IL 60544
Tatone Products Corp.
  1209 Geneva Ave.
  San Francisco, CA 94112
Techni-Models
  P.O. Box 9382
  Glendale, CA 91206
Testor Corp.
  620 Buckbee St.
  Rockford, IL 61101
V L Products
  7023-D Canoga Ave.
  Canoga Park, CA 91303
Williams Bros.
  181 Pawnee St.
  San Marcos, CA 92069
Wing Manufacturing
  P.O. Box 33
  Crystal Lake, IL 60014

FLYING MODELS AND ACCESSORIES

Aero Modeling
  6238 S.E. 15th
  Midwest City, OK 73110
Airborne Associates
  4106 Breezewood Lane
  Annandale, VA 22003
American R/C Helicopters Inc.
  23811 Via Fabricante
  Mission Viejo, CA 92675
Andrews Aircraft Model Co.
  P. O. Box 231
  Topsfield, MA 01983
Astro-Flight Inc.
  13377 Beach Ave.
  Venice, CA 90291
Blue Ridge Models
  P.O. Box 9188
  Asheville, NC 28805
Bob Violett Models
  26516 Aiken Drive
  Clarksburg, MD 20734
Bridi Hobby Enterprises
  1611 E. Sandison St.
  Wilmington, CA 90744
Bud Nosen Models
  P.O. Box 105
  Two Harbors, MN 55616
Carl Goldberg Models Inc.
  4734 W. Chicago Ave.
  Chicago, IL 60651

Cloer Industries
  P.O. Box 5810
  Security, CO 80931
Concept Models Inc.
  2906 Grandview Blvd.
  Madison, WI 53713
Cox Hobbies
  1505 E. Warner Ave.
  Santa Ana, CA 92702
Craft-Air
  7851 Alabama Ave.
  Canoga Park, CA 91304
Dave Platt Models
  2657 N.E. 188th St.
  Miami, FL 33180
D & B Model Aircraft
  6823-D Colonial Drive
  Mentor, OH 44060
Dodgson Designs
  2904 S.W. Camano Drive
  Camano Island, WA 98292
Du-Bro Products Inc.
  480 Bonner Rd.
  Wauconda, IL 60084
E & J Models
  P.O. Box 356
  Route 1
  Slatington, PA 18080
Exhib Air
  1955 S. 299th Place
  Federal Way, WA 98003
Fliteglas Models
  P.O. Box 324
  Route 1
  Neoga, IL 62447
Flyline Models
  2820 Dorr Ave.
  Fairfax, VA 22030
Gas Model Products
  9376 Wilcox Drive
  Cincinnati, OH 45239
GMC Models
  7349 Rindge Ave.
  Plaza de Rey, CA 90291
Guillow's
  40 New Salem St.
  Wakefield, MA 01880
Hi-Flier Manufacturing Co.
  510 E. Wabash Ave.
  Decatur, IL 62525
House of Balsa
  2814 E. 56th Way
  Long Beach, CA 90805
Jack Stafford Models
  12111 Beatrice St.
  Culver City, CA 90230
Jemco
  1305 Foothill Drive
  Vista, CA 92083

Jetco Models
  883 Lexington Ave.
  Brooklyn, NY 11221
Kavan Model Aircraft
  1424 E. Borchard Ave.
  Santa Ana, CA 92705
Lanier Industries, Inc.
  Briarwood Rd.
  Oakwood, GA 30566
Lees Hobbies
  11902 La Bella Ave.
  Sunnyvale, CA 94087
Lenco Products
  219 First St.
  Buchanan, NY 10511
Maco Model Aircraft Inc.
  694 Shadow Wood Lane
  Webster, NY 14580
M & P Enterprises
  Box 338
  Lone Oak, TX 75453
Mark's Models
  P.O. Box 2134
  Escondido, CA 92025
Master Kits
  6 Fox Rd.
  Plainville, CT 06062
Mexa Model
  P.O. Box 127
  Laredo, TX 78040
Micro Models
  P. O. Box 1273
  Covina, CA 91722
Micro-X
  Box 1063
  Loraine, OH 44055
Midwest Products Co.
  400 S. Indiana St.
  Hobart, IN 46342
M H Manufacturing
  2623 Honolulu Ave.
  Montrose, CA 91020
Model Engineering of Norwalk
  54 Chestnut Hill
  Norwalk, CT 06851
Model Rectifier Corp.
  2500 Woodbridge Ave.
  Edison, NJ 08817
Peck-Polymers
  P.O. Box 2498
  La Mesa, CA 92041
Peerless/Kyosho
  3919 M St.
  Philadelphia, PA 19124
Prather Products
  1660 Ravenna Ave.
  Wilmington, CA 90744
Proctor Enterprises Inc.
  P.O. Box 9641
  San Diego, CA 92109

R/C Kits Mfg.
353 Briar Ave.
North Canton, OH 44720

RCM Products
P.O. Box 487
Sierra Madre, CA 91024

Rev Model Products
430 Kay St.
Addison, IL 60101

R.M. Enterprises
3255 N.W. Crocker Lane
Albany, OR 97321

R/N Models
P.O. Box 2527
Lancaster, CA 93534

Royal Electronics Corp.
3535 S. Irving St.
Englewood, CA 80110

R & S Hobby Products Inc.
P.O. Box 61
Oak Lawn, IL 60453

S. C. Modeler
1999 Larkin Ave.
Elgin, IL 60120

Scientific Models Inc.
340 HY Snyder Ave.
Berkeley Heights, NJ 07922

SIG Manufacturing Co.
Montezuma, IA 50171

Soarcraft
Pacer Industries Inc.
1550 Dell Ave.
Campbell, CA 95008

Special Edition Plans
P.O. Box 2555
Schenectady, NY 12309

Sterling Models Inc.
3620 G St.
Philadelphia, PA 19134

Sure Flite Products
6475 Knott Ave.
Unit L
Buena Park, CA 90620

Top Flite Models
1901 N. Narragansett Ave.
Chicago, IL 60639

Tri R Models Inc.
1747 Rush Rd.
Wickliffe, OH 44092

Tyro Model Supply
P.O. Box 11511
Palo Alto, CA 94306

Vintage Aero
1 The Glen
Tenafly, NJ 07670

VK Model Aircraft Co.
12072 Main Rd.
Akron, NY 14001

Wes Craft Mfg.
P.O. Box 393
Calabasas, CA 91302

Williams Bros.
181 Pawnee St.
San Marcos, CA 92069

Windspiel Models
P.O. Box 459
Route 3
Coeur d'Alene, ID 83814

World Engines
8960 Rossash Ave.
Cincinnati, OH 45236

RADIO CONTROL

Cannon Electronics
13400-26 Saticoy St.
North Hollywood, CA 91605

Cirrus/Hobby Shack
18480 Bandilier Circle
Fountain Valley, CA 92708

Cox/Sanwa
1505 E. Warner Ave.
Santa Ana, CA 92702

EK-logictrol
3322 Stovall St.
Irving, TX 95061

Futaba
630 W. Carob St.
Compton, CA 90220

Heathkit
Heath Company
Benton Harbor, MI 49022

Kraft Systems Inc.
450 W. California Ave.
Vista, CA 92083

Litco Systems
P.O. Box 90
East Hanover, NJ 07936

MRC
Model Rectifier Corp.
2500 Woodbridge Ave.
Edison, NJ 08817

Royal Electronics Corp.
3535 S. Irving St.
Englewood, CO 80110

RS Systems
5301 Holland Drive
Beltsville, MD 20705

S&O R/C Products
23700 Bessemer St.
Woodland Hills, CA 91367

Specialist
Millicott Corp.
1420 Village Way
Santa Ana, CA 92705

Westport International Inc.
349 Boston Post RD.
Milford, CT 06460

Advice from the Experts

UNLIKE PRIZE-WINNING cooks and skilled magicians, model plane enthusiasts do not tend to keep secrets from one another. Expert modelers are usually very willing to divulge the ingredients and tricks they use to produce excellent planes.

There is more to building a model plane than manual dexterity, although that certainly is important. Equally important is ingenuity—the ability to develop new assembly and flying procedures as they become necessary.

Here are several tips from model aircraft fanciers who have been active in the hobby for a considerable period of time. They are provided to give beginners an idea of the kind of inventiveness that is so much a part of this entertaining pastime.

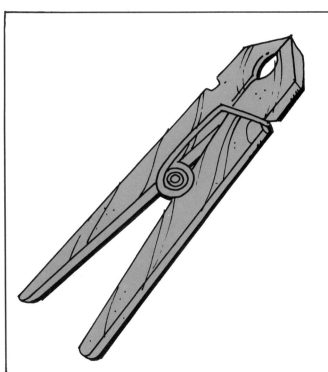

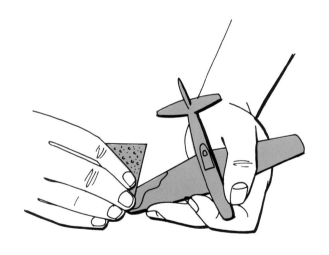

Spring-type clothespins are excellent for clamping small parts of a plastic kit together while waiting for glue to dry. To allow the clamps to grip well in tight corners, use a razor saw to trim away the outside corners of the jaw. This alteration will give the clothespin a "nose" like that of a pair of pliers.

Every plastic model you build will have tiny gaps where the parts do not fit together exactly. Fill these gaps with modeling putty, applied with a knife. Allow the putty to dry overnight and then sand with extremely fine-grit wet and dry sandpaper. Use only enough water to lubricate the abrasive action.

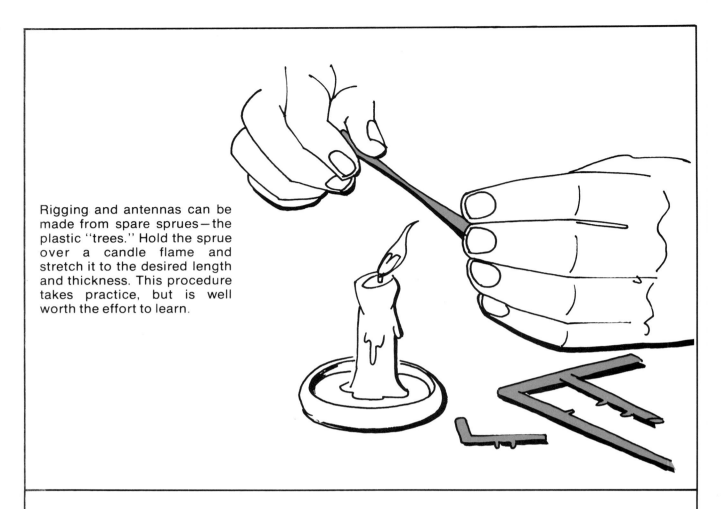

Rigging and antennas can be made from spare sprues—the plastic "trees." Hold the sprue over a candle flame and stretch it to the desired length and thickness. This procedure takes practice, but is well worth the effort to learn.

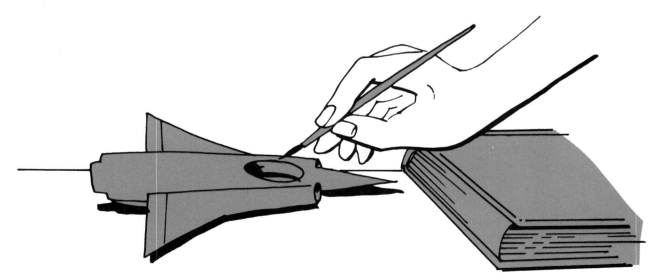

When painting a model with a brush, rest your hand on a book or other object that raises your hand above the level of the area being painted. You'll find that detailing is more precise.

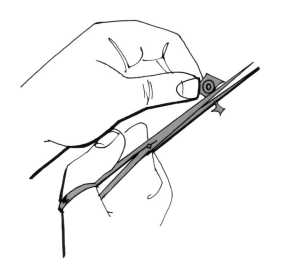

When applying decals, be sure to trim the paper backing very close to the design. This will eliminate the appearance of carrier film when the decal is applied. After soaking the decal, use tweezers to slide the insignia onto the plane's surface. Then use the tip of a facial tissue and your fingers to dab it into position.

Even though the sanded balsa wood surface of a glider wing may feel smooth to the touch, it is actually a mass of bumps and "hairs" that can increase drag. Applying a coat of dope seals the surface and makes the hairs stiff so they can be sanded off. To get a smooth, hard finish, apply successive coats of dope and sand the surface after each application.

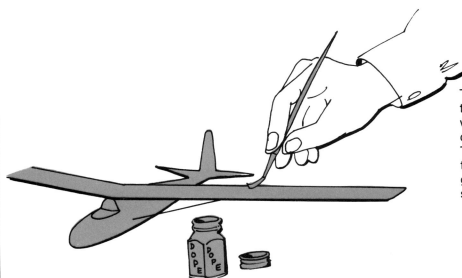

To avoid splitting and warping the wood of your glider, coat it with dope that has had a few drops of castor oil added to it. The oil gives the dope an elastic quality and will protect your glider better while keeping surfaces flexible.

You may be able to triple the altitude of a small handlaunch glider by launching it with a catapult made of four to eight strands of 3/16-inch rubber attached to a post driven in the ground. To use this launching method you must also add a wire hook to the bottom of the nose of your glider. A similar method, requiring a much longer piece of rubber, is used for very large gliders.

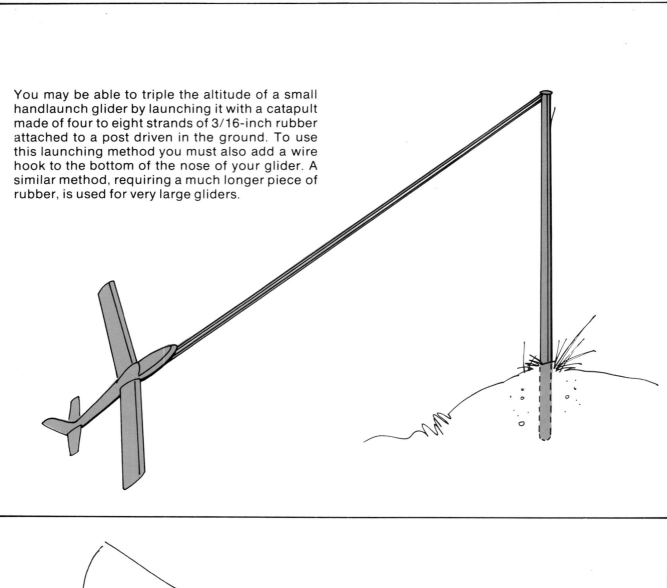

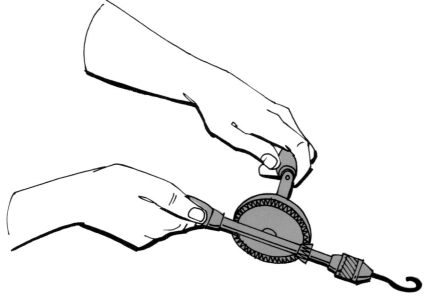

You can wind the rubber motor of an outdoor rubber-powered model plane more easily by using an ordinary hand drill. Simply attach a hooked wire, such as a piece of coat hanger to the drill and crank the handle. Make sure that the wire is securely attached to the chuck to prevent accidents.

To obtain the optimum number of turns in your rubber motor, stretch the rubber three to four times its normal length. Move slowly toward the nose of the plane while cranking the hand drill.

Rubber mounts should be lubricated for good performance. Never use lubricants such as castor oil, since they will cause the rubber to deteriorate. Instead, use a solution of green soap and glycerine. In warm weather, use six parts of glycerine to every four parts of tincture of green soap. A one-to-one ratio of green soap and glycerine should be used in cold weather.

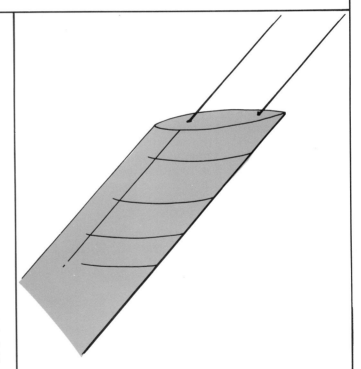

Run control lines through the wing whenever you can. This procedure reduces drag and eliminates the need for a line guide.

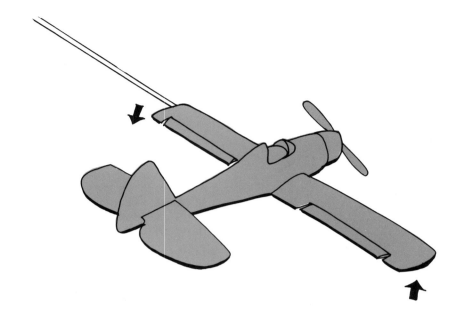

Make sure that your control line model flies with its wings parallel to the control lines under all circumstances. If your model tends to bank, it will land and take off on one wheel. If it banks toward you, the control line will slacken and you will lose control of the plane. You can stop unwanted banking by warping the trailing edge of the inboard panel down and the trailing edge of the outboard panel up.

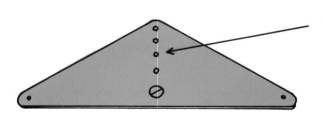

Overcontrolling is a common problem with new flyers of control line planes, and causes many crashes. To reduce the sensitivity of the controls, move the pushrod into a hole closer to the pivot point of the bellcrank. You can also reduce sensitivity by securing the lines closer together on the control handle.

Propellers of miniature engines should be trimmed and balanced before using in flight. Sand any bead of plastic you find on the edges of the blades. Then fit a shaft through the propeller hole and rest the shaft on two razor blades stuck into a wood base. Sand the heavy part of the blade until the prop balances horizontally. Be careful not to ruin the airfoil characteristics of the blade.

If your new engine becomes tight after a few slow runs, it is not necessarily "frozen." The tightness is probably caused by a buildup of "shellac" on the cylinder wall. Remove the cylinder and scour the inside wall carefully with fine or medium steel wool. Then wash, oil and replace. Use no material other than steel wool for this procedure; emery cloth and similar materials will damage the bore.

Avoid removing the head from a hot engine. A hot head will stick, and forcing it can damage the cylinder. If you must remove a hot head, first pour a small quantity of fuel over the head slowly to cool it off. Do not let the fuel touch the cylinder.

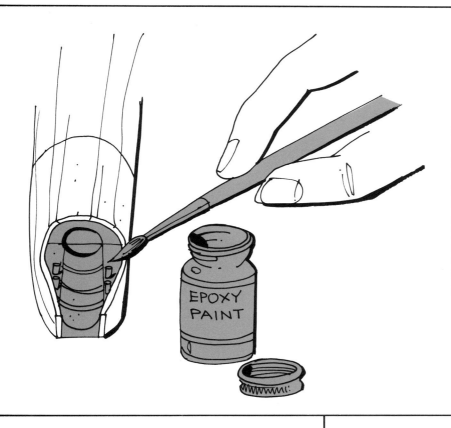

When building a radio-control airplane, make sure you fuel-proof the interior of the engine compartment and the surrounding area. This can be done with epoxy paint or an acrylic enamel, but marine fiberglass resin is a top choice of experienced RC plane builders. Make sure you seal every tiny crevice, and use the resin only in a well-ventilated area.

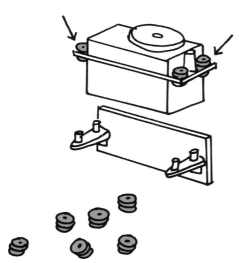

Screws and rubber grommets are used to secure the servo tray of an RC plane to the fuselage and the servo to the tray. The rubber grommets are designed to dampen engine vibration. Therefore, do not tighten the screws to the point where the grommets are compressed too much. This will defeat their dampening function.

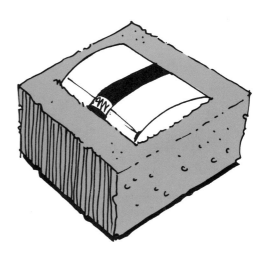

Never use foam rubber for the protective wrapping of the receiver and battery pack of an RC plane. It rebounds with the same force it absorbs and can cause damage to the components. Use only polyurethane foam or low-grade Styrofoam of the type used for protecting the contents of a box for shipping.

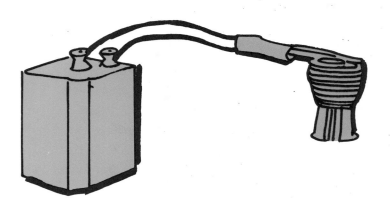

When an engine will not fire at all, remove the glow head and connect it to the battery clip. Watch the coil inside. If it does not become red hot, your problem is either a bad battery, incorrect connection or a malfunctioning glow plug.

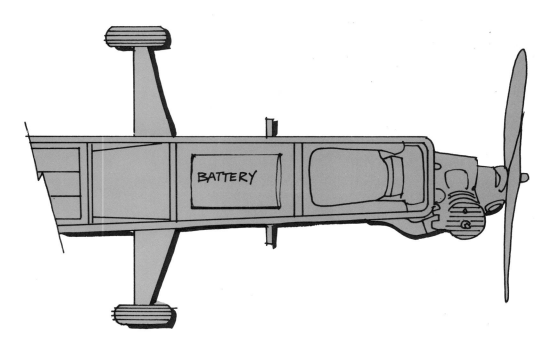

A radio-control plane should be balanced so that it is slightly nose heavy. When arranging the radio control components, always put the battery pack as close to the nose as possible, relative to the other components. If placed behind the other components, the heavy battery pack will move forward with enough force to damage components in its path during a crash.